Co

any mistakes please dont dump Books for respect to are lord,

or advice or donating Tel- 07936971116

Introduction

Islam is talked about all the time these days, but unfortunately convenient sound bites dominate at the expense of real information, leading to a distorted picture of what Muslims actually believe in or practice. IDCI receives numerous enquiries about various aspects of Islam all the time and therefore decided to compile this collection of frequently asked questions and answers in order to replace hearsay with facts. The booklet's intention is to inform; it wants to provide sound and well-researched answers to whoever seeks to know the truth about Islam and Muslims, as well as enable Muslims to respond to similar questions they may receive from friends, colleagues or neighbours. To do so, we have tried to keep the answers brief, yet support them with evidence from the source texts of Islam – the Qur'an and the Sunnah [see below for definitions] – and without getting into the finer detail or potential controversies. There is ample literature available on each of the topics covered to facilitate further study, therefore, this guide is only intended to provide an overview. We sincerely hope that it will help in dis-spelling misconceptions as well as attempts to discredit Islam due to ulterior motives. Whether one agrees with the Islamic viewpoint or not is a matter of choice and faith. However, the decision should be taken on the basis of validated information rather than polemics. Armed with this booklet the reader is therefore also empowered to assess whether a media report mentioning Islam or Muslims is genuine or biased or whether a politician's conclusions in relation to Islamic concerns are based on fact or fiction. We have selected the questions which in our experience are most frequently on people's minds, yet inevitably other questions will remain unanswered, so if you have a question you do not find covered on these pages, do not hesitate to write to us. We might even choose to include it in a future edition of this booklet.

What does Islam and Muslim mean?

Unlike most other religions, which were named after their founder or the community following it, Islam is not associated with a person, people or country but named in accordance with what it stands for: submission to the Creator. A related word of the Arabic word *"Islam",* meaning submission, is *"Salam",* meaning peace. A Muslim, a follower of Islam, is a person who strives to attain peace with themselves and their surroundings by submitting to the guidance provided to them by their Creator through revelation. This guidance includes certain truths, a Muslim believes in, and certain actions they follow. By being defined in this manner, Islam is open to all, irrespective of place, cast, race, nation etc. According to the Qur'an (5:3) it is the way of life chosen by God for mankind:

"Today I have completed your religion for you and perfected My favour upon you and am content with Islam (submission) as a religion for you". (Al-Qur'an, 5:3)

What is the purpose of life according to Islam?

According to the Qur'an, Allah is;

"The One who created death and life to test you as to who does the best deeds, and He is the mighty and forgiving." (Al-Qur'an, 67:2)

"And I (Allah) did not create Jinn and mankind except to serve Me." (Al-Qur'an, 51:56)

Hence the purpose of life on earth is two-fold: A temporary time and space to test our conduct and whether we serve Allah alone. For our earthly existence, Allah gave us everything we need and more, and we owe Him our gratitude which we express through prayer and by acting in accordance with His guidance. Since we cannot repay Him for His favours, we are expected to share and pass these on to those who are less fortunate than ourselves. According to the prophet Muhammad (peace be with him), the best Muslim is he who is most beneficial to those around him.

Who do Muslims worship and why?

Central to Islam is the belief in one unique and supreme divine being as the creator of all life known to us – Allah - and therefore being the only one worthy of worship. He has no equal nor any partner in divinity. To worship Him is the ultimate purpose of all that has been created, as He says in the Qur'an:

"And I (Allah) did not create Jinn and mankind except to serve Me." (Al-Qur'an, 51:56)

And, "This is Allah, your Lord, there is no god but Him, the creator of everything, so serve Him, and He is a protector of everything." (Al-Qur'an, 6:102)

Therefore, Islam rejects the worship of anything else as idolatry. Muslims worship Allah directly without intermediaries, and this is what they invite others to, as the Qur'an states:

"Say, oh people of the Book (Christians and Jews), come to a common word between us and you that we serve none but Allah and do not associate anything with Him nor take each other as overlords instead of Allah. Then if they turn away, say: Be witnesses that we have submitted."

(Al-Qur'an, 3:64)

This strict monotheism of Islam is expressed in Surah (Chapter) 112 of the Qur'an:

"Say: He is Allah alone, Allah, the everlasting, He does not reproduce nor has been reproduced, and nobody is a match for Him." (Al-Qur'an, 112:1-4)

Muslims reaffirm this truth in their daily prayers by reciting the opening Surah (Chapter) of the Qur'an:

"Allah is praised, the Lord of all worlds. The Owner and Giver of Mercy. The King of the Day of Repayment. We serve only You and ask only You for help. Guide us on the straight path. The path of those You have favoured, Not of those deserving anger, Nor of those who lose their way."

(Al-Qur'an, 1:1-7)

Who is Allah?

Allah is the name of the single and unique Creator of all existence. He is above and beyond His creation and does not become part of it, nor can we ever perceive or understand Him due to the limitation of our senses. God does not become man, nor can man become God, the Creator and His creation are fundamentally different and not alike. However we can describe Him through some of His characteristics or attributes, such as Merciful, Powerful, Just, Forgiving etc., and strive to emulate those. The name Allah is not exclusive to Arabic, in the Aramaic New Testament, for example, it is "Eli" and *"Elohim"* (Arabic: *"Allahumma"*, meaning oh God, dear God). In Surah (Chapter) 112 the Qur'an describes Allah as follows:

"Say: He is Allah alone; Allah the everlasting; He does not reproduce nor has been reproduced; and nobody is a match for Him." (Al-Qur'an, 112:1-4)

And: "Allah, there is no God but Him, the Living, the Eternal. Neither slumber nor sleep overtake Him. Whatever is in the heavens and on earth is His. Who will intervene in His presence without His permission? He knows what lies before them and behind them, and they don't grasp any of His knowledge except what He permits. His footstool is as wide as the heavens and the earth; maintaining them does not tire Him, and He is the exalted and great." (Al-Qur'an, 2:255)

What is the Qur'an?

The Qur'an is the direct word of Allah revealed in the Arabic language. Prophet Muhammad (peace be with him) received the revelation from the archangel Gabriel and then recited it ad verbatim to those around him. Its style is entirely different from his normal speech and its narrative, structure and rhythm are unique, which is why we find the following challenge in the Qur'an:

"And if you have doubts about what We (Allah) have revealed to Our servant (Muhammad), produce a similar Surah with the help of anyone you like besides Allah, if you are truthful. But if you don't do that - and you can never do it - then beware of the fire promised for those who reject (the truth), which is fuelled by people and stones."

(Al-Qur'an, 2:23-24)

The Qur'an was revealed to the prophet Muhammad (peace be with him) over the course of 23 years, often in relation to events of the time. The individual parts of the Qur'an were then both memorised and written down at the time of revelation together with the order in which the verses were arranged. Considering this fact, the Qur'an is an even more amazing and astonishing book, for if we imagine stringing together news articles over 23 years we would not expect them to become a cohesive book with a coherent and consistent as well as timeless narrative, another characteristic pointed out in the Qur'an itself:

"Do they not reflect on the Qur'an? If it were from other than Allah, they would have found many contradictions in it." (Al-Qur'an, 4:82)

Soon after the Prophet's death the existing copies of the Qur'an were compiled by his companions into a master copy. Muslim and non-Muslim scholars agree that the Qur'an read by Muslims today is identical to that read at the time of the prophet, leaving no room for doubt about its authenticity as with other scriptures, which were transmitted only orally to start with or whose original language (e.g. Aramaic for the New Testament) no longer exists. The Qur'an describes itself as a book of guidance and serves as inspiration for Muslims in their daily lives:

"This Book contains without doubt a guidance for those who beware (of Allah)." (Al-Qur'an, 2:2).

It is left to people's own choice whether they want to follow that guidance:

"We have revealed to you the book for mankind with truth, so whoever wants to be guided, does so for his own good, and who goes astray, goes astray against himself, and you are not a guardian over them." (Al-Qur'an, 39:41)

Who is Muhammad and what is a messenger?

Muhammad (peace be with him) is the last, or seal, of a series of messengers chosen by Allah for the guidance of their respective people or mankind at large. Although divine messengers remain ordinary humans who do not claim divinity for themselves, the task of delivering the divine message and demonstrating by example of how it should be followed entails a heavy responsibility and thereby makes the messengers special people who deserve the highest of respect, which is why Muslims always send peace and blessings upon them whenever their names are mentioned. As the final messenger, Muhammad (peace be with him) is the universal guide to mankind for the remainder of time:

"Muhammad is not the father of any of your men but the messenger of Allah and the seal of the prophets, and Allah knows all things." (Al-Qur'an, 33:40)

"And We only sent you as a mercy for all the world."
(Al-Qur'an, 21:107)

In the Qur'an we are told to believe in all the messengers who confirmed each other in their respective missions:

"Say: We believe in Allah and what has been revealed to us and what has been revealed to Ibrahim (Abraham) and Isma'il (Ishmael) and Ishaq (Isaac) and Ya'qub (Jacob) and the tribes and what was given to Musa (Moses) and 'Isa (Jesus) and the prophets from their Lord, we make no difference between any of them, and we submit to Him."

(Al-Qur'an, 3:84)

Of course, it is not for us to choose one above the other; instead we are meant to follow the messenger sent to us, just as one would follow an updated operating manual of a manufacturer rather than opting to use an earlier one. The Qur'an states:

"You have in the messenger of Allah a beautiful example for whoever hopes for Allah and the last day and remembers Allah a lot." (Al-Qur'an, 33:21)

In Islamic terminology, the messenger's example to be followed is called the *"Sunnah"*. Combined, the Qur'an (the divine scripture, see above) and the *Sunnah* (see below) make up the source of guidance and rulings in Islam.

Is Muhammad mentioned in other religious scriptures?

All divine scriptures and all divine messengers emanate from the same source and therefore confirm each other, although the guidance was adapted by our Creator as mankind evolved. Not all scriptures are preserved in their original state, not least because many early scriptures were only passed on orally and not recorded in writing at the time of their revelation, allowing alterations and misunderstandings to develop over time. Many of the scriptures given to a specific messenger make reference both to the messengers who came before and those to come after. Therefore, references to the final messenger, Muhammad (peace be with him), are found in many scriptures, and recognised as such by those who read them with an open mind not constricted by dogma.

The references in the Bible are manifold, although Christians and Muslims will usually interpret them differently. In Songs of Solomon, 5:16:

"His mouth is most sweet; Yea, he is altogether lovely. This is my beloved, and this is my friend, oh daughters of Jerusalem."

The words **"altogether lovely"** are a translation of what in the Hebrew text is pronounced as **"Muhammadim"**. One of the clearest announcements of the prophethood of Muhammad (peace be with him) is found in Deuteronomy (5th Book of Moses), 18:18-19, where God is said to have told Moses:

"I will raise up for them a prophet like unto you from among their brethren; and I will put my words in his mouth, and he shall speak to them all that I command him. And whoever will not give heed to my words which he shall speak in my name, I myself will require it of him."

He is to be raised *from among their brethren;* so he does not belong to the House of Israel, but to the descendants of Ishmael, his brother. He shall speak to them *all that I command him,* he will utter words, which *he shall speak in my name.* We know that the revelation of the Qur'an began with "Recite in the name of your lord" (Al-Qur'an, 96:1), and with one exception the heading of all Qur'an Surahs (Chapters) is "In the name of Allah, the merciful, mercy-giving". Muhammad (peace be with him) transmitted Allah's word in His name, and did not speak in parables like Jesus did, at least according to the Bible's testimony.

He is to be a prophet like Moses. As it is said: *"I will raise up for them a prophet like you..."* Now, after him, only Muhammad (peace be with him) brought a complete code of Law, like Moses, as it is clearly stated about Jesus in Matthew 5:17: *"Think not that I have come to abolish the law and the prophets; I have come not to abolish them but to fulfil them."* Deuteronomy (5th book of Moses), 34:10-12 also confirms that Jesus could not have been the foretold prophet who was like Moses. It reads:

"And there has not arisen a prophet since in Israel like Moses, whom the Lord knew face to face, none like him for all the signs and the wonders which the Lord sent him to do in the land of Egypt, to Pharaoh and to all his servants and to all his land, and for all the mighty power and all the great and terrible deeds which Moses wrought in sight of all Israel."

All these characteristics, however, agree with what we know about Muhammad (peace be with him) who was raised in the House of Ishmael: he was Allah's beloved friend whom He brought near in the *Mi'raj* (the rising to the seventh heaven after *Isra*, the night journey from Makkah to Jerusalem), and whom He made strong and full of mighty power.

In the New Testament in Matthew, 21:43 Jesus warns:

"Therefore I tell you, the kingdom of God will be taken away from you and given to a nation producing the fruits of it."

John 14, 16-17 mentions the *"Counsellor"* to be sent after Jesus. Counsellor is a translation of the Greek *'parakletos'*, a word used for helper, follower. It gets easily confused with the Greek word *'periklytos'* which can be rendered as praiseworthy and is in sense identical with the Arabic word Ahmed. The Qur'an tells us in this respect:

"And when 'Isa (Jesus) the son of Maryam (Mary) said: oh children of Israel, I am the messenger of Allah to you, confirming what came before me of the Torah and giving you good news of a messenger to come after me whose name is Ahmad..." (Al-Qur'an, 61:6)

Bearing this in mind, Jesus is said to have stated, in the Gospel of John, 14:16-17:

"And I will pray the Father, and he will give you another Counsellor, to be with you for ever, even the Spirit of truth, whom the world cannot receive, because it neither sees him nor knows him; you know him, for he dwells with you, and will be in you."

This is about someone whom Allah will send after him and who will stay with them forever. In a double sense Muhammad (peace be with him) dwells with us for all the time. Firstly, as he is the last prophet forever, and we will therefore follow his example forever, and he will not be replaced. Secondly, as the message transmitted by him, the Qur'an, will stay unchanged with us all the time.

Christians prefer to associate these words with the Holy Spirit, and this interpretation is added in John, 14:22-16:

"Judas (not Iscariot) said to him, "Lord, how is it that you will manifest yourself to us, and not to the world?" Jesus answered him, "If a man loves me, he will keep my word, and my Father will love him, and we will come to him and make our home with him. He who does not love me does not keep my words; and the word which you hear is not mine but the Father's who sent me. "These things I have spoken to you, while I am still with you. But the Counsellor, the Holy Spirit, whom the Father will send in my name, he will teach you all things, and bring to your remembrance all that I have said to you."

This confusion arises due to the 4th century dogma of the Trinity, but whatever has been told in these verses about the Counsellor does not match what the Bible says about the Holy Spirit. Mark, 12:36 states: *"David himself, inspired by the Holy Spirit, declared…"* The Holy Spirit was thus already present with the former prophets and can hardly be another counsellor to be sent to the people after Jesus. Customarily the term Holy Spirit is used for the Angel Gabriel who brings revelation from God.

John, 16:1-15 is quite clear:
"Nevertheless I tell you the truth: it is to your advantage that I go away, for if I do not go away, the Counsellor will not come to you; but if I go, I will send him to you. And when he comes, he will convince the world concerning sin and righteousness and judgment: concerning sin, because

they do not believe in me; concerning righteousness, because I go to the Father, and you will see me no more; concerning judgment, because the ruler of this world is judged. 'I have yet many things to say to you, but you cannot bear them now. When the Spirit of truth comes, he will guide you into all the truth; for he will not speak on his own authority, but whatever he hears he will speak, and he will declare to you the things that are to come. He will glorify me, for he will take what is mine and declare it to you. All that the Father has is mine; therefore I said that he will take what is mine and declare it to you.'"

The foretold prophet *"will not speak on his own authority, but whatever he hears he will speak"* – a clear indication of the Qur'anic revelation. And he will glorify Jesus by correcting the image that he was God incarnate whereas he himself clearly stated: *"the word which you hear is not mine but the Father's who sent me"*.

The Hindu Puranas contain prophesies of a man called Mahamad to appear in Arabia to fight evil. It has also been said that the "Kalki Avatar" foretold in Hindu scriptures as a saviour to come refers to the prophet Muhammad (peace be with him). Because these texts date even further back in time, the controversies regarding their correct translation and interpretation are even more pronounced than with the Bible. In the internet age there is now a wealth of easily accessible material available on the subject and the above therefore only serves as a pointer for those who wish to research the matter further.

What is the Muslim belief about Jesus and Moses?

Jesus and Moses are the two prophets sent directly before the prophet Muhammad, peace be with them all. Both were sent to the Israelites and neither claimed to have been a universal prophet (Jesus, for example, is said in the Bible to have stated that he was only sent to the lost sheep of the House of Israel, and that he was sent to uphold, not to change the law). Their stories are recounted in the Qur'an as an example for believers. The Qur'an also sets the record straight on the issue of the Trinity, which became Church dogma more than three hundred years after Jesus. It states that Jesus never claimed divinity for himself but always admonished people to worship only the One God who had sent him as a messenger. Muslims also believe in the immaculate conception of Mary who had her child implanted by the archangel Gabriel, and that Jesus did not die on the cross but was raised to Allah to return as the Messiah near the end of time.[1]

What is the Sunnah? What is a Hadith?

A *Hadith* is a report about something the prophet Muhammad (peace be with him) said or did. Collectively, the Prophet's example is called the *Sunnah*. Together with the Qur'an it constitutes the source of Islamic rules about all aspects of life.

"You have in the messenger of Allah a beautiful example for whoever hopes for Allah and the last day and remembers Allah a lot." (Al-Qur'an, 33:21)

1. For more information on the Islamic view of Jesus and Moses see the IDCI publications **"Moses, Jesus, Muhammad... 3 Men:1 Mission"** and **"For they killed him not: A Muslim Portrayal of Jesus"**, available free on request.

The *Sunnah* is important because it demonstrates how the guidance in the Qur'an can be put into day-to-day practice. To ensure that a report attributed to the prophet is authentic, Muslim scholars developed a unique science of examining the chain of transmission (*isnad*) of any report claiming to be from the Prophet combined with a thorough analysis of the reliability of those within that chain who relayed his words (*'Ilm ar-Rijal*). All human effort is fallible, but on the whole it represents a very robust system.

What is the Shariah?

The *Shariah,* Arabic for the path or the method, is the legal system of Islam which governs all aspects of human life with regards to rights and duties, obligations and prohibitions. It is based on the Qur'an and the *Sunnah* (see above), from which detailed rulings are derived by means of reasoning, analogy and legal consensus. Thus the *Shariah* has a similar division of statute and case law as Western law, with the exception that the statute is not a man-made constitution but a divine revelation.

What is the Muslim creed?

In accordance with the teachings of the prophet Muhammad (peace be with him) a Muslim believes in Allah, the Angels, Books and Prophets of Allah, life after death with paradise and hell, the weighing of the deeds on the Day of Judgement, and divine predestination. The most important starting point for these beliefs is the oneness and uniqueness of Allah, the only God. Amongst His creatures, besides us, are the angels who serve Him without the free will given to humans. To communicate His guidance to mankind He sent revelation (books, scriptures) and messengers (prophets) to warn about the life after death and final judgment. Muslims also believe that everything and its outcome, good or bad, is predestined by Allah as for Him, the limitations of space and time (past and future) which determine our lives do not apply.

What does Islam say about mercy and forgiveness?

Christian preachers often claim that Christianity is a religion of love whereas Islam is a religion of rules and regulations, although the word love occurs more frequently in the Qur'an than it does in the Bible. Contrary to such claims the God of Islam is a merciful God – the chapters of the Qur'an commence with reminding us of His mercy: "In the name of Allah, the Merciful, the Mercy-Giving", and in the Qur'an Allah states:

"…My punishment, I will afflict with it whom I will, and my mercy extends to everything…" (Al-Qur'an, 7:156)

Accordingly we have been informed by the prophet Muhammad (peace be with him) that Allah declared that *"My mercy prevails over my anger"*. Out of this mercy, He keeps the path of repentance and forgiveness open for all:

"And when those who believe in Our signs come to you, say: peace be with you, your Lord has prescribed mercy for Himself so that if any of you does evil ignorantly, then repents afterwards and does good, He is forgiving, merciful." (Al-Qur'an, 6:54)

Thus Allah declares to the believers:

"Oh you believers, if you beware of Allah, He will provide a break-through for you and cancel your bad deeds from you and forgive you, and Allah possesses immense generosity."

(Al-Qur'an, 8:29)

And to those who don't believe in Him:

"Say to those who reject (the truth), if they stop, they will be forgiven what went before, and if they return, then the example of old has already passed." (Al-Qur'an, 8:38)

And, "Say: oh My servants who have been extravagant against themselves, do not despair of the mercy of Allah, for Allah forgives all sins, for He is the forgiving, merciful."

(Al-Qur'an, 39:53)

The attributes of Allah are also there for us to emulate, hence Muslims are encouraged to forgive and show mercy, which the Qur'an describes as one of their strengths:

"And whoever is patient and forgives, that is one of the firmest things (to do)." (Al-Qur'an, 42:43)

This forgiveness should be extended to those who are not Muslims as advised in the Qur'an:

"Tell those who believe to forgive those who do not hope for the days of Allah, so that He may reward people in line with what they did." (Al-Qur'an, 45:14)

What does Islam say about life after death?

Many people live oblivious of their purpose and the consequences of their actions, claiming that they "only live once". The Qur'an makes reference to this erroneous belief:

"And they say: there is only our worldly life, we die and live, and only time destroys us, and they have no knowledge about it, they only presume. And when Our clear signs are recited to them, their argument is only that they say: bring our forefathers if you are truthful. Say: Allah gives you life, then He makes you die, then He gathers you to the day of resurrection in which there is no doubt, but most people don't know." (Al-Qur'an, 45:24-26)

Belief in a life after death is a central element of the Islamic faith. Islam views life on earth as a temporary testing ground for the conduct of every individual. The overall result of an individual's work and effort will not be available within this life but subject to divine judgment after one's death and resurrection. The Day of Judgement provides the ultimate justice which is not attainable on earth. Based on their record, individuals will either be granted an eternal life of bliss in paradise or condemned to eternal punishment in hell. It is then that those condemned will wish they had another chance, but the cycle cannot be repeated.

"Until when death reaches any of them, he says: my Lord, send me back, so that I do good work in what I left behind; no way, it is only something he says, and behind them is a barrier until the day of resurrection. Then when the horn is blown, there will be no connection between them on that day and they will not ask each other. So whose weight is heavy, those will be successful. And whose weight is light, those will have lost themselves, they will remain in hell."

(Al-Qur'an, 23:99-103)

What does Islam say about heaven and hell?

"…this worldly life is only a provision, and the hereafter is the lasting abode. Whoever does bad, he will only be rewarded with the like of it, and whoever does good, male or female, and is a believer, those will enter the garden where they will be provided for without counting."

(Al-Qur'an, 40:39-40)

Life on earth is temporary, followed by death, resurrection and judgement, based on which each soul is given its place according to its deeds. Whilst there are stages in the hereafter, dependent on one's detailed actions, there will essentially be two groups, those who have passed the test and are rewarded, and those who failed and are punished.

"This is a reminder, and for those who beware (of Allah) is the best destination. Gardens of Eden with the doors opened for them." (Al-Qur'an, 38:49-50)

The gardens of paradise are an eternal place of peace with delights beyond what one could ever imagine in this material world.

"For no soul knows what comfort is hidden for them as reward for what they used to do." (Al-Qur'an, 32:17)

The key to entering paradise is belief in Allah as the sole creator and sustainer of all life. Those who reject this truth and His guidance, on the other hand, will have had their full recompense already in this life and will have no reward in the hereafter as stated in the Qur'an:

"Whoever wants the fruit of the hereafter, We increase its fruit for him, and whoever wants the fruit of this world, We give him of it and he has no share in the hereafter. There final and eternal abode is hell-fire." (Al-Qur'an, 42:20)

"So it is, and for the transgressors will be the worst destination. Hell, which they will enter, a bad place to be."
(Al-Qur'an, 38:55-56)

Are all rules in Islam of equal importance?

As a complete system of guidance, Islam naturally has rules for all areas of life. Some people suggest that it is possible to apply them selectively, giving more importance to certain rules and belittling the importance of others. Such relativism ultimately erodes the whole structure of the system designed to help us to live righteous personal and social lives. This approach is akin to someone claiming that it is less important to observe a no entry sign in the highway code than a stop sign. Both signs are means to avert potential danger, and it would not be possible to arrange them in a hierarchy. The same applies to the rules in Islam.

What are the consequences of disbelief or denial?

The Qur'an makes it quite clear, that to accept divine guidance, as well as the consequences of doing so or not, are every individual's own choice:

"Whoever wants to be guided is guided for his own good and who goes astray, goes astray only against himself, and no-one burdened will carry another's burden, and We never punish until We send a messenger." (Al-Qur'an, 17:15)

This verse also clarifies that nobody is held to account for making this choice until the message has first reached them. Regarding the choice to accept guidance, there are different categories of people: Those who believe in it will have the reward for following it, whereas those who reject it, knowing it to be the truth, will be punished accordingly in the hereafter as will those who were simply careless about it or who pretended to follow the guidance for some ulterior motive without really believing in it. Allah's judgment is always just. Considering that it is He who brought us to life in the first place, He has an absolute right to be appreciated and paid heed to. To do otherwise is a crime against our very nature as human beings and the purpose we were created for. All actions have consequences, but these do not always manifest themselves immediately, and in His mercy, Allah provides for everyone, whether they acknowledge Him or not, but in the next world requires an account of what we did with the gifts He gave us.

What does Islam say about human rights?

The universal declaration of human rights is not quite as universal as the name suggests as it is not free from the cultural prejudices of its time when it was issued after a devastating war in Paris in 1948. It is hailed as a milestone in that its scope reaches well beyond the rights afforded to citizens in the American Declaration of Independence or to a select group of noblemen in Magna Carta, yet it is restrained by the political concept of the nation state and thus not universal in the true sense. Almost 1500 years ago, however, the prophet Muhammad (peace be with him) granted minorities in the city state of Madinah statutory rights which were not limited to only a chosen few. Based on the Qur'an, Islam has the concept of the **"rights of Allah"**, these are inalienable rights of every individual which, if violated, are an offence against God Himself. They include the right to life and property and freedom of belief as well as the protection of a person's dignity and reputation, which is still missing from the human rights catalogue presently subscribed to by Western nations.

What does Islam say about parental rights?

Parents are held in high esteem in Islam as they are to be given respect by divine command:

"And We admonished man to be good to his parents. His mother carried him in discomfort and gave birth to him in discomfort, and carrying and weaning him takes thirty months, then finally when he reaches full strength and reaches forty years he says: my Lord, grant me that I am grateful for your blessings which You have blessed me with and my parents and that I do good work which You will be pleased with, and make my children good for me, for I turn to You and am of those who have submitted (as Muslims)." (Al-Qur'an, 46:15)

"And your Lord decreed that you should serve none but Him and show kindness to parents. If one or both of them reach old age with you, then do not say words of irritation to them nor scold them but speak to them with respect. And give them comfort in humility out of mercy and say: my Lord, have mercy on them as they looked after me when I was little. Your Lord knows best what is within you. If you are righteous, then He is forgiving to those who repent."

(Al-Qur'an, 17:23)

What does Islam say about gender equality?

The concept of equality is often misunderstood. In Islam, all human beings are of equal worth, everybody, old or young, rich or poor, male or female, has direct access to Allah through prayer without intermediary, has access to His divine guidance and will be judged on their individual merit. At the same time, all people are different, and an egalitarianism which wants to remove all differences and level all individuals to fit a common denominator is neither beneficial nor realistic. The Qur'an states:

"And do not wish for what Allah has favoured with some of you above others; for men there is a share of what they have earned and for women there is a share of what they have earned, and ask Allah of His favour for Allah knows all things." (Al-Qur'an, 4:32)

As for men and women, they were created physically different and discharge different roles within society, something which does not detract from their equal value as expressed in the Qur'an:

"For men and women who submit (as Muslims), and men and women who believe, and men and women who are humble, and men and women who are truthful, and men and women who are patient, and men and women who are devote, and men and women who are charitable, and men and women who fast, and men and women who guard their chastity, and men and women who remember Allah often, Allah has promised them forgiveness and a tremendous reward." (Al-Qur'an, 33:35)

Both men and women have rights upon and duties towards each other:

"And women have similar rights as they have duties, but men are one stage above them, and Allah is mighty and wise." (Al-Qur'an, 2:228)

The latter is because in Islam, women are entitled to protection and men are obliged to cater for them as expressed in the Qur'an:

"Men look after women on account of what Allah has favoured some of them above others and of what they spend from their property...". (Al-Qur'an, 4:34)

"And the believers, men and women, are protectors of each other.." (Al-Qur'an, 9:72)

Within society, Islam frowns upon the free mixing of sexes and does not condone for a non-related mixed couple to spend time alone, both because of the obvious temptation but also to protect the woman from the man taking advantage and the man from a false accusation. Islam also wants both men and women to have their own spheres in addition to the shared sphere of life. This is something, Western society is also slowly coming to accept, with women, for example, demanding women-only car park sections, at least at night, for extra security, as well as other segregated facilities.

What does Islam say about marriage, adultery and fornication?

Marriage is the union of a man and a woman for the purpose of establishing a family and a condition for an intimate relationship. It is the state of being united as spouses in a consensual and contractual relationship recognised by civil or religious law and therefore does not only safeguard the interests of the spouses but also their wider families and, especially, their offspring. In Islam, marriage is a sacred institution which comes about by a civil contract witnessed publicly. Adultery is when a married person entertains an intimate relationship outside marriage, and fornication is when an unmarried person does so, and Islam forbids both. Marriage is the foundation of the family, which in turn is the foundation of society, it provides stability and certainty of lineage, and therefore Islam restricts sexual relationships to the setting of marriage.

The Qur'an warns us about extra-marital sex due to its harmful consequences: "And do not go near fornication, for it is indecency and a bad way." (Al-Qur'an, 17:32)

Why does Islam permit polygamy for men but not for women?

Islam permits men to marry up to four women (polygyny):

"...then marry from the women permitted to you, two, three and four, and if you fear that you cannot be fair, then one..." (Al-Qur'an, 4:3)

Although this is the exception, not the rule, as the Qur'an also requires them in the very same verse to treat their wives equal yet warns that this is not easily achieved:

"And you will not be able to act justly between women even if you tried..." (Al-Qur'an, 4:129)

This permission takes care of a number of problems which arise for women both at a personal and a society level, for example the imbalance of genders after a war, where mostly men are killed, or the common situation in the West of a married man taking a mistress but not treating her and his wife equal nor giving her the security of marriage. Since marriage is a precondition for intimate relationships in Islam, a second relationship is only permitted by way of marriage and with the approval of the first wife. Another case, which was the reason for some of the marriage contracts of the prophet Muhammad (peace be with him) is to be able to provide a home and security for widows who could otherwise be left to have to fend for themselves. If only monogamous relationships were permitted, this would not be possible without a man first divorcing his existing wife, an unlikely scenario when the intention is to help a woman bereft of a husband.

The reverse situation of a woman having more than one husband (polyandry) is not permitted, not only because of the different psychological needs of men and women, where a man can generally look after more than one woman, but a woman finds it difficult to commit to more than one man, but moreover in the interest of clarity of parentage. Whilst DNA testing has made it possible to establish fatherhood, it is not universally available and also often requires the consent of both parties, which can be denied. A child has the right to know who his/her biological parents are; in a polygynous relationship, this is still easy to establish without recourse to testing, but not so in a polyandric relationship.

What does Islam say about homosexuality?

Islam does not approve same-sex marriages since one of the purposes of marriage is procreation and same-sex couples cannot have children by natural means. As explained above, a marriage does not just regulate the rights and duties of spouses, but also needs to serve the interests of the children resulting from this union. As a consequence, Islam forbids homosexual relationships outright, just as it forbids any other sexual relationships outside marriage. In doing so, Islam does not specifically discriminate against homosexuals, since the prohibition applies across the board. A man attracted to a man, or a woman attracted to a woman, is asked to practice abstinence in the same way a man or woman attracted to someone else's spouse or two unmarried people of the opposite sex are asked to do so.

What is the Islamic dress code for men and women?

The Qur'an describes the rules for public dress code and conduct:

"Tell the believing men to lower their eyes and guard their chastity, that is purer for them, for Allah is informed of what they get up to. And tell the believing women to lower their eyes and guard their chastity and not to display their beauty except of what is apparent, and to throw their head coverings over their chests…" (Al-Qur'an, 24:30-31)

The purpose of this advice is to ensure that the public sphere, which is shared by men, women and children, is free from sexual enticement and such attraction is restricted to the privacy of people's homes, where these restrictions are relaxed. Modern society has become highly sexualised, which leads to young, yet immature people entering into unstable relationships before being ready to commit to marriage, and can tempt adults who would otherwise be in a stable relationship into a destructive temporary fling. Islam places a high value on family and its rules are designed to prevent situations which endanger the family as the basic building block of society. Islam also expects men to dress and act like men and women to dress and act like women, and men growing a beard is part of keeping their natural appearance.

What does Islam say about music and dancing?

It is a widespread misconception that Islam is a very serious religion which prohibits any kind of entertainment. Children sing at school and adults have songs, often with a religious content (songs of praise), to make manual work less monotonous, for example during harvest. People beat the drums and dance at weddings. The key difference between entertainment sanctioned by Islam and modern music and dance culture is that the boundaries of decency must be maintained at all times. What is not condoned is mixed dancing in public or songs and dance moves of an erotic or sexually enticing nature of the kind presently dominating, for example, music videos, because such forms of entertainment can have a corrupting influence upon the youth and also represent an exploitation of women whose bodies are paraded for public viewing.

What does Islam say about racism?

In the Islamic story of creation, the devil was ejected from paradise for disobedience to Allah due to racism when he said:

"I am better than him, You created me from fire and created him from clay." (Al-Qur'an, 38:76)

The prophet Muhammad (peace be with him) said: *"Allah does not look at your faces or wealth but looks at your hearts and deeds."* He also said in his sermon during his farewell pilgrimage: *"All mankind is from Adam and Eve, an Arab has no superiority over a non-Arab nor a non-Arab has any superiority over an Arab; also a white has no superiority over a black nor a black has any superiority over white except by piety and good action."*

In Islam, a person's distinction is not by virtue of his origin but by virtue of his conduct:

"Oh mankind, We have created you from male and female and made you into clans and tribes so that you know each other. The most honoured amongst you before Allah is the most aware (of Him) amongst you, for Allah is knowing and informed." (Al-Qur'an, 49:13)

What does Islam say about the rights of neighbours?

In Islam, social responsibility is very important. For example, the prophet Muhammad (peace be with him) said that *"He is not a Muslim, who eats his fill whilst his neighbour goes hungry."* In Islam, charity starts at home, so the first group of people entitled to ones' support and kindness is one's household and immediate family, then the extended family, then the nearby neighbours followed by the more distant neighbours. In this mutual support system, all are responsible for each other's welfare, and this principle applies irrespective of whether a neighbour is also a Muslim or not.

What does Islam say about the environment?

In the Islamic understanding, humans do not own the earth but have been given a privileged position on earth as its guardians or trustees. This includes being mindful of how we use its resources:

"...and do not waste, for He does not love those who are wasteful." (Al-Qur'an, 6:141)

By way of example, the prophet Muhammad (peace be with him) taught that even if one had a river flowing past, one should not take from it more water than necessary. An abundance of a particular resource should not encourage wasting it. Islam discourages excess and encourages conservation. On the issue of waste, the Prophet also taught that *"cleanliness is part of faith"*. Sadly, this environmental awareness, together with spiritual awareness, has been in decline in many Muslim countries after they had been colonised by the West but is gradually experiencing a revival.

Why does Islam prohibit alcohol and other narcotic drugs?

"I was drunk and didn't know what I was doing" is a commonly heard excuse in countries where drinking alcohol is a culturally tolerated practice or even encouraged as a key ingredient of socialising. The consequential costs for society are enormous from road death through domestic violence to health expenditure. In Islam we are held accountable for our actions both in this world and the next, and therefore anything which alters our state of mind and thereby impairs our ability to make rational decisions is prohibited. As alcohol and drugs take effect, they also cloud an individual's judgment as to how intoxicated he or she is, causing people to drink more than they can handle and drive or operate machinery under the influence of alcohol or drugs or make sexual advances they later regret. For this reason Islam advocates a total prohibition so that whatever ultimately has an intoxicating effect is prohibited outright in any quantity.

"Oh you believers, narcotic drugs and gambling and idolatry and divining are filth from the work of the devil, so shun it in order to be successful. The devil wants to place enmity and hatred amongst you with narcotic drugs and gambling and to divert you from the remembrance of Allah, so will you stop?" (Al-Qur'an, 5:90-91)

Why is Islam against lending money at interest/ usury?

"Allah destroys interest and gives increase to charity, and Allah does not love anyone ungrateful and sinful."

(Al-Qur'an, 2:276)

Islam puts the common interest before the individual interest. If someone is facing hardship and needs to borrow, it is immoral to take advantage of his situation and profiteer from a mark-up. Interest also has a destructive effect on the overall economy, causing inflation and foreclosures, because any enterprise which would make enough return to pay its resources and workers would have to earn an additional percentage to satisfy the demand of the lender. This becomes ultimately unsustainable unless there is constant growth and expansion, one of the key reasons for wars of expansion in the past, and it is impossible for any organism to grow indefinitely. Thus interest becomes a cancer which eventually kills the host as the debt accumulated through compound interest (where interest not only has to be paid once on the original sum but is also added to all subsequent outstanding interest charges) becomes unpayable. Today most nations are indebted beyond a single generation's capacity to pay. What is worse is that the money owed was never fully backed by real wealth but consists of mere book entries (fiat money), an arrangement which allows a bank to lend a multiple of its own assets yet demand payment in full and in kind if a borrower defaults. Thus the sums owed by all the nations of the world are greater than the wealth created by these nations and the imbalance can only be redressed by a major collapse, bringing hardship and suffering to all but a few. Islam, on the other hand, advocates charity instead of hoarding, as the cumulative effect of charity is that in the long run everybody is better off.

What does Islam say about animal welfare?

Islam teaches kindness to people and to animals and does not permit us to abuse of the power we have over other creatures. Killing animals is permitted where they pose a danger and also for food. The prophet Muhammad (peace be with him) is reported to have said:

"There is no person who kills a small bird or anything larger without just reason, but Allah, the Mighty and Sublime, will ask him about it." It was said: 'O Messenger of Allah, what does just reason mean?' He said: 'That you slaughter it and eat it, and do not cut off its head and throw it aside.'"

Islam demands that animals, including those it permits to be killed for food, are both treated and dispatched humanely. In the modern consumer society we live in, everything is sanitised in order to make us buy; we are not meant to see suffering, blood, disease, death – we have institutions to hide any human suffering which could get in the way of the perfect shopping experience, and meat is presented to us neatly packaged as if no animal had ever been killed in the process. At the same time we are encouraged to consume in large quantities leading to conveyor belt slaughter which is anything but humane. For the convenience of the automated processes in the slaughter house, animals are rendered unconscious prior to slaughter by either captive bolt or electric stunning. Nobody can really argue that being knocked on the head by a heavy implement or being electrocuted is particularly humane. In the diet of the prophet Muhammad (peace be with him) meat was a complimentary item, not as staple food. To be truly considered as *halal* – permissible – animals had to be treated well during their lifetime – akin to organic farming – as well as slaughtered humanely, which means not to be slaughtered in front of each other, not subjected to any cruelty or unnecessary violence, and a cut to be made with a razor-sharp implement to sever the wind pipe and the jugular vein. When we cut ourselves accidentally with a razor or sharp knife, we do not feel the pain straight away. As a result of the cut, which leaves the spinal cord intact, the brain is starved of oxygen, leading to imminent unconsciousness, whilst the heart keeps pumping blood, removing toxins from the body. If done properly, the animal remains calm throughout until muscular convulsions set in a couple of minutes later, whilst the animal has long been unconscious. It is these convulsions that are mistaken by many for a sign of suffering and why some animal rights campaigners demand that the animal be rendered unconscious through stunning first. It is a fact that a significant proportion of stunned animals recover subsequently before the cut is made (known in the industry as mis-stunning), therefore subjecting these animals first to the blow or electric shock and then, after having regained consciousness being slaughtered hanging upside down on a conveyor belt. What animal rights campaigners fail to realise is that not the Islamic *(halal)* or Jewish (kosher) methods of slaughter are inhumane, but the automation processes of mass slaughter. Since Muslims in the industrialised countries also now demand meat on their plate every day, Islamic slaughter houses also have adopted mass methods of slaughter, and some even pre-stunning, at the expense of animal welfare.

Why does Islam prohibit eating pork?

As the creator and designer of human beings, Allah knows what is good for us and what is not, and He says:

"Oh you believers, eat from the good things which We have provided for you and give thanks to Allah if you truly serve Him. He has only forbidden you carrion, blood and pork and whatever has been consecrated for other than Allah. But whoever is forced without (wilful) transgression or habit is not to be blamed: Allah is forgiving and merciful."

(Al-Qur'an, 2:172-173)

Muslims, therefore, rely on the divine wisdom in observing these prohibitions, which does, of course, not stop them trying to find out why certain potential food sources are prohibited. Whereas with alcohol this is more straight-forward, as the harmful effects of intoxication can easily be observed, it is less obvious with foods which do not develop symptoms immediately. In the past it was thought that the prohibition was due to the risk of tape worms, which is greater in pork than in any other meat, but recently, through DNA studies, it has been observed that the structure of pig cells is very similar to that of human ones – which is why pig organs are used for transplants as they are the least likely rejected –, and if this is true, eating pork almost comes close to cannibalism. Another reason why pork might be considered unclean is that a pig's diet is not strictly vegetarian but can even include faeces and their own young, and a key prohibition in Islam is meat from predatory animals or scavengers.

How does Islam prove the existence of God to an atheist or agnostic?

Whereas the philosopher Immanuel Kant went as far as proving the rational necessity for the existence of God, the actual existence of God is a matter of faith and cannot be proven, because the realm of God is not accessible to us humans given our sensory limitations. Likewise, the non-existence of God is a matter of faith which cannot be proven, nor can it be proven whether there is life after death or not, for nobody has yet come back from the dead. One could, of course, argue with an atheist that if there was just a great void after death, a believer would be no worse off than a non-believer, but if there indeed is a God meting out judgement, then a non-believer will certainly be worse off than a believer. For somebody willing to listen and observe, there are undoubtedly endless pointers to a greater existence than our temporary time on earth. A complex creation such as life on earth in all its amazing forms requires a creator as it would be highly irrational to assume that it all came about by itself and pure chance. The agnostic position is a little more honest in that it is an admission by someone that they don't know or aren't sure, but it also is akin to shrugging one's shoulders as if the question didn't really have any relevance and did not matter with regard to how we live our lives. The truth is that a person who knows to be accountable at a later date will try to lead a more righteous and moral life. Whilst the issue ultimately comes down to personal belief, what is not acceptable to Muslims is that atheists try to pretend that they hold the objective, unbiased neutral ground, because theirs is as much an unprovable conviction as that of the believer.

Is the Qur'an compatible with modern science?

In Islam, knowledge is divided into two types: revealed knowledge and acquired knowledge. Islam encourages Muslims to seek knowledge and form a sound understanding of the world around them, which is how Islam laid the foundation of modern science in geography, medicine, chemistry, astronomy as well as the methodology of research, teaching and learning. However, Muslims also acknowledge that there are realms of knowledge to which we have no direct access and therefore need to rely on revelation.

Modern science relies exclusively on empirical knowledge (acquired through sensory experience using observation and experimentation) and develops theories deducted from it. Our senses, however, are limited by the material time and space environment we live in and do not provide answers to questions relating what may lie beyond. Thus, science can deliver answers of how the universe developed after it first came into being, but not how it came into being in the first place as its origin obviously lies outside itself. The Qur'an contains numerous facts which could not have been obtained by the rudimentary means of knowledge acquisition available at the time of its revelation but have since been confirmed as accurate by modern science.

For example, water as the building block of all life:
"Do those who reject (the truth) not see that the heavens and the earth were a continuous canvas, then We separated them and made from water every living thing, do they then not believe?" (Al-Qur'an, 21:30)

The trajectories of stars and planets:
"And He is who created the night and the day and the sun and the moon, each travels in an orbit." (Al-Qur'an, 21:33)

Or that the body of the Pharaoh of the time of Moses would be preserved: (Addressed to the Pharaoh) "So today We rescue your body to be a sign for those after you, and many people are careless about Our signs." (Al-Qur'an, 10:92), when it was mummified and buried long before the time of, and far away from, Muhammad (peace be with him) and only discovered long after he passed away.

Following the age of colonialism, after Western science had won its confrontation with the Christian church and started to replace religion as an allegedly more rational way to look at life, Muslims apologetically claimed that Islam and the Qur'an were entirely compatible with science and even tried to explain passages of the Qur'an in a manner to agree with latest scientific theory, although those theories would sometimes turn out to be incorrect and replaced by others. Since the revelation of the Qur'an represents divine knowledge, the approach to measure it by the benchmark of science is flawed. Instead, the validity of a given scientific theory needs to be tested against the standard of the Qur'an to determine whether it is sound or not.

What does Islam say about the theory of evolution?

The theory of evolution, taught by science as a form of religious dogma today, is baseless in many of its assumptions. Whilst its key tenets have never been proven, it gained popularity because biological evolution was translated into social evolution and used to justify the conquest of less evolved cultures during the age of European colonialism. That life in all its complexity came about by pure chance in the time available is a mathematical impossibility and a claim more ludicrous than that if you dropped a million words at random into a word processing program they would eventually assemble themselves into a meaningful book of history or literature. Nor would a heap of metal or plastic parts abandoned in a garage somewhere miraculously re-assemble into a fully functioning machine. When we humans develop a piece of art or technology, we take full credit for its creation, yet the much more amazing creation of the universe and life on earth are taken for granted as not having required any kind of conscious order and design. It is an easily observable fact that order does not develop from chaos without purposeful intervention, rather chaos develops as soon as order is no longer maintained. Likewise, the world we know came about and is maintained by the divine will and intervention. This does not dispute the fact that in the realm of biology there are mutations and adaptations, however, these are limited to take place within a given species. No substantive evidence has ever been produced about inter-species evolution, such as a reptile evolving into a bird. The smallest mosquito is in itself a complex design which could not have evolved from any other organism. The fossil record evolutionists initially used to rely on in support of their theory does not contain the expected intermediate life forms to prove mutation from one species to another. The "missing link", talked about since the theory of evolution first gained popularity for political reasons, remains missing.

How do Muslims view other religions?

All true religions originally have a divine origin and essentially taught the same message: to worship the Creator alone and to excel in good conduct. However, most religions have been distorted over time through the forgetfulness, jealousies, ambitions and manipulations of their adherents and functionaries. Religious practices relying entirely on oral transmission were more prone to such alterations than those with a written scripture, but scriptures, too, were often changed through translation and through interpretations being added to the text. The Qur'an is the only divine book which has been preserved in its original form in writing since its earliest days – for one and a half millennia by now. Muslims therefore respect the texts and protagonists of other religions, but judge their validity exclusively against the benchmark of the Qur'an. The Qur'an issues the following call to those who follow earlier religions:

"Say, oh people of the Book (Christians and Jews), come to a common word between us and you that we serve none but Allah and do not associate anything with Him nor take each other as overlords instead of Allah. Then if they turn away, say: Be witnesses that we have submitted."

(Al-Qur'an, 3:64)

Was Islam spread by the sword?

This is one of the accusations frequently voiced against Islam by those concerned with its continuous growth in numbers. To start with, Islam as a religion still keeps growing today at a time when Muslims are in a weak position and the majority of refugees, due to wars imposed on them from outside, are Muslims. The criticism is also difficult to accept when the 20th and 21st centuries were the ones with the most extensive bloodshed through warfare in all human history. Islam is not a pacifistic religion and permits Muslims to defend their lives and country. In the early history of Islam, Muslims fought off attacks and in turn conquered the countries of their attackers. Other countries were opened to Islam through trade. What is important to note is that a military conquest did not imply the forced conversion of the population who were permitted to continue to practice their religion (Islam having been the first system which permitted religious minority rights) and granted them protection of the state in return for a protection tax (whilst exempt from military service and the annual Zakat payment applicable to Muslims). This fact is evident in the large numbers of Jewish and Christian minorities still living in the Middle East after centuries of Islamic rule and the survival of the Hindu and Sikh religion under Muslim rule on the Indian subcontinent. Since Islamic conduct requires conviction and hypocrisy is frowned upon, there would be little point in forcing anyone to become a Muslim. As the Qur'an puts it:

"There is no compulsion in religion. Right and wrong are self-evident. One who rejects idols and believes in Allah holds on to a reliable link which cannot break, and Allah listens and knows." (Al-Qur'an, 2:256)

What does Muslim fundamentalism mean?

The term fundamentalism was first coined to describe Christians who take the Bible too literally. It was later applied to Muslims mainly as a derogatory term to insinuate that they were fanatics and could not be taken seriously except maybe as a potential danger. This was at the time when Islam was built up in the West as the external enemy replacing the old foe of communism. The term is not in much use anymore, as it has now become commonplace to refer to Muslims as terrorists in order to define them as a menace.

What does Islam say about terrorism?

Terrorism is the exercise of indiscriminate violence to further political ends. It is a result of irregular warfare in which a small group of combatants uses tactics such as ambush, sabotage, or hit-and-run tactics as well as punishing civilians for the actions of their governments and military. Islam, which governs both the private and public sphere of life, has strict rules on combat, permitting warfare only for the purpose of defence and prohibiting combatants from involving or harming civilians. Thus Islam categorically prohibits terrorism. However, with the demonisation of Islam in public discourse by governments wanting to portray

Muslims as a threat as well as justifying the plundering of the resources of often defenceless Muslim countries, the term terrorism has been used very loosely. The same violence perpetrated by any group of people is described as terrorism or not dependent on whether those people are considered friends or foes. Thus it no longer matters whether an act is justifiable or not, but who commits the act. By condoning violence of allies and decrying even legitimate resistance by an enemy as terrorism, the term itself has been devalued and often even been used by various sides to justify the exercise of state terror. Islam permits a people to defend themselves against attacks on their property or lives, but teaches that any action taken must be proportionate. Islam does not permit aggressive acts of violence and holds every life as sacred:

"On account of that we prescribed for the Children of Israel that whoever kills a soul other than (in retaliation) for a killing or for a crime on earth, it is as if he had killed all mankind, and whoever revives one, it is as if he had revived all mankind, and Our messengers came to them before with clear proofs, after which many of them were wasteful on earth." (Al-Qur'an, 5:32)

What is Jihad or "holy war" in Islam?

Jihad is an Arabic word for struggle and effort in order to please Allah. It is applied both to personal effort aimed at an individual's improvement of character, "And strive in the way of Allah with true effort..." (Al-Qur'an 22:78), as well as armed struggle in the defence of land, freedom and honour. Islam permits Muslims to defend themselves against aggression as well as to take revenge for injustice committed against them, but places restrictions on the form and extent such action may take.

"And fight in the way of Allah those who fight you, but do not transgress. Allah does not love the transgressors."

(Al-Qur'an, 2:190)

Warfare is an unfortunate fact of life, and as with all other aspects of life, Islam regulates and moderates it, for example, by ensuring that non-involved civilians are not caught up in a battle nor livestock and natural resources harmed. The mass killings of this and the last century, which have witnessed the most brutal and indiscriminate wars of human history, can never be regarded as a mark of civilisation and would not be permissible under Islamic rules.

What solution can Islam offer to unite humanity and create peace in the world?

In the early days of Islam, the new Muslim community applied the guidance of the Qur'an and the prophet Muhammad – peace be with him – both in their private and public lives. The result was a civilisation whose cultural advancement left a rich heritage still resonating with us today. Whenever Muslims (and mankind at large) moved away from the divine guidance, they created problems for themselves; whenever they returned to it, they managed to reform their society. This still holds true today. Modern Western society is the outcome of the victory of science over the religious dogma of the Christian Church which was at odds with the knowledge gained from research and discovery. Initially perceived as liberating, the secular dogma which replaced the religious dogma has led to the greatest essentialist crisis since human history, with mass alienation, endless and ruthless wars, drug addiction, suicide, sexual licentiousness and perversion, loss of identity and purpose and nihilism. Islam, which has a much more holistic view of life and is not weighed down by the baggage of a futile antagonism between religion and science, can, by focusing on sound conduct, unite mankind in the worship of a single creator, eliminating man-made sources of conflict, such as national pride, elitism, arrogance, jealousy and exploitation. To do so, Muslims would need to return once more to the guidance of the Qur'an and the Prophet Muhammad (peace be with him), and apply this not selectively but wholeheartedly, making Islam once again a complete way of life in all its philosophical and practical aspects, rather than a disjointed set of dogmatic rules chosen by various factions in order to score points over their rivals. This can only be achieved once success in the hereafter becomes more important to the individual than success in this temporary world.

Why do Muslims say that every child is born a Muslim?

By stating that every child is born in a natural pure state of being (*fitrah*), Islam holds the opposite view to the teaching of the Christian churches that children are born shouldering the "original sin" and require baptism to be saved from damnation. The natural inclination of a human being is to be in wonder of the glory of creation and to acknowledge and call out to a supreme being, and it is only through education and socialisation that children are moulded into the various religions of their parents or society. For this reason converts to Islam often refer to themselves as "reverts" to highlight that they have freed themselves from false doctrines and returned to a more natural state of being. In Islam, children are considered innocent to start with and fully accountable for their actions only when they become adults.

How does a person become a Muslim?

A person becomes a Muslim by declaring the *"Shahadah"* (witness statement) that *"There is no god but Allah and that Muhammad is His messenger."* By this affirmation of Allah as the only deity entitled to worship, a Muslim rejects all false idols, and by attesting to Muhammad (peace be with him) being a messenger he also confirms all books and messengers of Allah before him. Having made this commitment, a Muslim then strives to practice Islam through the Five Pillars of Islam: To continue to be a witness to the oneness of God and the prophethood of Muhammad (peace be with him), to pray regularly, to give the obligatory charity, to fast annually during the fasting month of Ramadan, and to perform the pilgrimage to the Ka'bah in Makkah at least once during his/her life.